THE LIFE OF THE FOUR STOMACHS

The Life
Of The Four Stomachs

for Doris

Marilyn Gear Pilling

Marilyn Gear Pilling

October 4, 2006.

Black Moss Press
2006

Published by Black Moss Press at 2450 Byng Road, Windsor, Ontario, Canada N8W3E8.

Library and Archives Canada Cataloguing in Publication

Pilling, Marilyn Gear, 1945-
    The life of four stomachs / Marilyn Gear Pilling.

Poems.
ISBN 0-88753-426-0

    1. Women--Poetry. I. Title.

PS8581.I365L53 2006   C811'.54   C2006-902624-6

Cover art: The Residence of Peter McKerrall, Esq., Concession 5, Lots 15-16, Chatham Township, Kent County, Ontario (detail). *The Illustrated Historical Atlas of Essex and Kent Counties*, 1881

Design: Karen Veryle Monck

Black Moss Press acknowledges the generous support of the Canada Council and the Ontario Arts Council for its publishing program.

Le Conseil des Arts | The Canada Council
du Canada | for the Arts

ONTARIO ARTS COUNCIL
CONSEIL DES ARTS DE L'ONTARIO

Published and printed in Canada.

for Dan Pilling,
the Little Workshop & J. S. Porter

who knows, of the world,
only this salt this green this chewing:
the life of the four stomachs.

Contents

The Life Of The Four Stomachs

The Life of the Four Stomachs.. 11
Understanding T.S. Eliot at Last.. 12
Pea Season 14
Lilacs.. 15
At the Corner of James North and Vine... 16
Vulva is the Latin Word for Ditch... 18
Why Would Garrison Keillor Wash his Hands Ever? 19
After the Reading, Julie and Sheila Sleep Over 20
Some Mystery Must Remain.. 21
Domestication
    i.   little dishes in the street... 22
    ii.   overheard at the pharmacy 23
    iii. the tongue 24
    iv. star 25
    v.   this dog of yours 26
Cows 27

Hip Man

Hip Man 31
Every Living Minute 32
Six Months.. 34
Books 36
Letter Meditation by Water... 37
A Child Made of Snow.. 39
One Incarnation 40
In a Felled Tree.. 41
Pilgrimage to Prades 42
Alchemy 43
My Dear... 44
The Listener 45

Now You Are Mostly Gold And Blue

The Farm Your Lover 49
Spit.. 50
A Tale 51
Leave the Water In.. 53
Father... 54
Upstairs.. 55
Gold and Blue... 57
After Reading Margaret Atwood's *Negotiating with the Dead* 58
The Strands of that Fragrance 60
Last Story.. 61
The Spatula 62
Flora's Bread 63
Knowing Only Now Why I Asked... 64
Dear God 65

Domesticity

The Marriage
    i.   still life.. 69
    ii.   imprint 70
    iii. fire 71
    iv. deep in the hold 72
    v.   inline skaters 73
    vi. i am not ironing linen.. 74
    vii. gift 75
Her Daffodil Hair Flies with the Spring
    i.   two.. 76
    ii.   nine 77
    iii. eleven 78
    iv. twelve 79
    v.   fourteen... 80
    vi. seventeen... 81
    vii. nineteen 82
    viii. twenty-three.. 84
    ix. twenty-six.. 85

The Writer 87
Notes.. 89
Acknowledgements.. 90

The Life Of The Four Stomachs

that porous line
where my own body was done with
and the roots and the stems and the flowers
began.

Mary Oliver, *White Flowers.*

The Life Of The Four Stomachs

She lazes sun stunned, stone dumb
as spring wind rips through buttercups,
she grazes, rasps the saltlick with strong tongue,
knows of the world only this salt this green this chewing:
the life of the four stomachs.

On hot summer days, she drowses under the maple tree
with her kind, haunches abutted, bellies
hugging the dreaming earth, on the road of their
backbones shadow dapple, light at play.

She waters at the river as light leaves
the sloping fields of hay,
hooves sunk in muck, slosh
of tepid water lapping,
scatter of minnows.

You and I have never lived
the life of the four stomachs.
You know only my mind.
You do not know the vowels of my silence
the tall consonants of my arms, how they feel
around you, the verbs of my finger tips
touching the whorls of yours.
You have never known the language
of my sleep, have not felt
my eyelashes sweep your palms of intent
or the span of my hand on the cage of your ribs.
You have never lain in bed with me peeling an orange.
You have not eaten the red veined flesh of the dark plum.
You have not tasted the salt of my pores or my tears.

There is a way to know me.
You only have to let the soft animal of your body
love what it loves.

Understanding T. S. Eliot At Last

> *breeding*
>
> *Lilacs out of the dead land*

It's not just the wind in magnolia
changing bride to plain girl
not just the wind turning puddles
from mirror to muddle sway

It's not just the lurid green
that bursts from the ditches
the snares of branches
crouched crimson in the fields

It's the hot sap of my own quickening
scalding stasis from my silver linings
it's the peepers that trill
from the murk of my swamp

It's not just the green flames
that burn the earth
the leaves that unfurl in flawless faith
the birds mad with love

Not just the jack in the pulpit
that pops overnight
the brazen stink of skunk cabbage
or mustard lust of buttercup

It's that in spring the grass is blue
wind blows it into shimmer
On all sides it tarantellas forth
to where the earth's in waiting for the sky

It's that the wind
that rushes from banished desire
thrusts me out
into waves of grass, blue blowing

It's that the fandango ratcheting up in my heart
takes two

Pea Season

It is pea season here in Ontario
as the last days of my career laze by.
Office door open, to all appearances working,
but in my lap, under the desk, quart boxes of peas in the pod.

Crack open, strip, spill, eat, pod after pod after pod,
it takes on a rhythm I cannot break even when sated
their taste that first green of unfurling leaves.

Building up in my lap, a grand pile of pods
a swelling surround of green.
Getting out will entail a flailing, a splitting, a splaying.
Sometimes I chew the pods too,
spit the ribboned remnants out.

I have eaten thirty-four boxes so far this pea season.
My father used to do this, my daughter once ate
a six quart basket of peas in the pod at one sitting,
a genetic trait that coils down the generations,
all of us gorging on the core of spring,
a green that is tender, unrepeatable, a presence
so relentless a princess knows it is there
under her mattress.

There are peas that must be picked and eaten urgently
for toughness and tastelessness, thug brothers
wait in the wings.
Peas so tiny they're almost invisible
their taste the most divine of all.

Hands busy, mouth full, body trance that swallows mind,
in the last days of my career but already in the pasture.

Lilacs

How you plant the kitchen stool beneath them, climb on top, tip
    your head back, reach towards heaven, wobble
        in a swim of scent that nearly drowns you,
           sever.

The cascade of memory catches in your hair on the way down
    instantly you see your mother and her sisters, the three of them
        looking a little old-fashioned now, house-dresses
           of tiny, flowered print, home-done perms.

You gather them, the purple panicles, the fresh green hearts,
    the little twigs, your mother and your aunts,
        gather them from the ground as you
           would gather harvest grasses, armfuls and armfuls.

You bring them in, whelm of their scent against your face
    settle them in the kitchen, blue delft pitcher
        living room, periwinkle jug
           bedroom, white-flowered china vase.

You let them saturate the air you breathe
    knowing where they will take you
        knowing what you risk.

At The Corner Of James North And Vine

Coming from the market to my car, I stub my toe and it hurts
so much that I want to lie down on the pavement and howl
      but on I trudge as if nothing has happened
         trundling my red buggy behind me.

In the parking lot booth is a note that says Back Soon. Most days
I would be mad to find a note where soon is open-ended like life,
      peeved to wait to get my deposit back, especially
         if I had just stubbed my toe. Yet today I stand

by my car like a donkey in the sun and make a mental list of why
I'm not annoyed. Because against my chest is a bag of peas in the pod
      a bag with the heft of a good-sized dog.
         Because I am taking a pod from the bag

cracking it open with practiced motion, stripping the peas
eating them one by one, enjoying the look of my long silver nails
      the rings on my fingers. Because one of the rings is the milky
         blue of the saltlick the cattle lapped when I was a girl

long ago on the farm. Because my toe I now see, as I stretch my neck
to look over the bag, has begun to ooze dark blood and this has replaced
      my pain. Because the air holds a tang of cool and the sky
         is bigger and bluer than ever, the sun the kind of sun

that will always shine. Because it is the first of July, a beginning.
The man comes back. He is grizzled. Ninety years old or so. He looks –
      the word was made for him – shriven. Does not owe me money.
         Today it costs five dollars to park for one hour.

Why? Because the Jehovah Witnesses are in town, he says.
I accept this and open my bag to offer him peas in the pod
      to show that no matter how many he takes
         there will be plenty, that peas are like loaves

and fishes. He helps himself to as many pods as his bony left hand can hold
for his right is full of tickets and keys. In my country, he says, there is
     a saying: *When a beautiful woman offers you vegetables,*
          do not fast. Here is a man, ninety years old or so

and still flirting! I show him my toe, how the small pale nail pokes out
from a collar of livid red. I am sorry, he says, how did it happen?
     The peas, I tell him. I could not see where I was going
          for the bag of peas in the pod.

He nods. Smiles a grave smile. On his lower gum a crowd
of teeth pile towards the centre, some sit on the shoulders
     of the others, all press forward, lean out to see
          this world, its bony hands both empty and full.

Vulva Is The Latin Word For Ditch

auprès de La Roche d'Hys

After Howard's picnics
of red wine, brie, baguettes
the others go to view the local
sights, while I stretch out
in a ditch behind the car,
doze nose to nose with
coquelicots, nestle next to
thistles. Down here, deep
in the Lilliputian life,
small rustles, tickles, buzz
and hum, the denizens of
ditches used to intrusions –
empty bottles holding ruddy
sweetish glaze, a wine
fuzzed Canadian – *n'importe*
quoi. Ants adjust their route
to climb the curving hill
I have become, spiders drop
their glinting lines, two dark
blue dragonflies perform
on wild lace. This is where
the Burgundian sun stores
her warmest concentrate
this is where the languorous
light sends innuendo,
this is the only place allowed
to go ungroomed, here
unseen in the browse and tangle
this is where the mischief can begin.

Why Would Garrison Keillor
Wash His Hands Ever?

*on looking at Garrison Keillor's photograph,
a head shot more fingers than face*

The fingers are long and crowded together, five of the nine
      within range of his nose.

After long puzzling, I get it. He's found his day on his fingers.
      He's smelling the chives he weeded that morning
            the tomato vine he pinched off, the basil he picked later
                  the onions he chopped, the garlic he crushed
                      his own cum.

Why would Garrison Keillor wash his hands ever
      when simply by letting his fingers crowd close
         to his nose like this
               he can be in the buzzing, pullulating garden
                   potentilla brushing his thigh,
         he can be naked in the candor of his lover's exposure
while the photographer shoots his photograph.

After The Reading, Julie And Sheila Sleep Over

Someone on high has given this snowglobe a mammoth shake
      the god of loaves and fishes, maybe
          the god of mountaintops.

The kitchen fills with white light, snow flakes tip and turn
      from that glass dome on high, they drift, feint, flip
          onto their backs so the god of loaves and fishes
              can admire their cold shining bellies.

Inside the snowglobe, Julie in flannelette pajamas, Sheila wrapped
      in wool sweater, I in pilling green housecoat,
          we three entranced by each frosty finn, each intricate gill,
          each unique dreaming eye.

On the table, coffee clementines cheese toast
      our talk of mothers brothers children lovers
          hidden thoughts out on the table
              now homely and harmless as toast crumbs.

Endless falling spell of snow
      the unfamiliar taking shape
          heaven's bread fallen to earth
          mounds of new risen hush.

Some Mystery Must Remain

at the festival of art & spirit concert
St. Jerome's University, July 2003.

Beside me, a strawberry blonde and her licorice brunet
      lover, his hand on her thigh, his arm closely coated
with hairs of shiny black. Her arm beside his, soft fuzzy
      peach in the sacred light that streams from the notes of
Lamentations and Praises, Learned of Angel, Sanctus.

She shifts position, her culotte slides up, reveals a leg
      so hirsute, black hairs so thick and so coarse
I seem to be viewing an animal's pelt. Though the foot
      at the end of the limb is shod in a white, flowered
shoe, I follow the line of the leg to see if it somehow

belongs to the boyfriend brunet – it doesn't, of course –
      then crane to check the roots of her hair, her brows
her lashes behind glasses – all true strawberry blonde.
      Dona Nobis Pacem, Agnus Dei, The Awakening –
in the midst of Spirit, this irruption of feral leg.

Domestication

i. little dishes in the street

In an outdoor café in Budapest my sister
tells me that in Canada
she is afraid of dogs but in Buda she is not.

Here in the old world multitudes of
dogs without owners
run in the streets. These dogs are like

people, she says, their gaits purposeful
you can almost see the briefcase
in their jaws, jumping up or biting

seems the last thing on their minds,
they give way when they
meet you, as any polite stranger would.

There are little dishes in the streets, she says
dishes left by older folk
who feed the dogs of Budapest.

A waiter or perhaps a Count disguised
stops at our table
white apron over black dress pants,

tilts a silver pot, sends steaming
streams into our cups.
From a tiny silver pitcher, I add cream,

consider the dogs of Canada, those
my sister fears,
chained, muzzled, *Beware* nailed overhead.

ii. overheard at the pharmacy

It was George says the first woman you know George George
wouldn't hurt a flea you've met my dog George.

Oh yes says the second I've met George yes George is lovely George
did **that**?

I move to where I can see her.

Between her nose and mouth and on her chin
crazy crisscross, black stitches scoring angry red
a face no art will ever restore.

Yes believe it or not and he'd just the day before got his
papers I've been taking him to be trained to do
therapy at the nursing home
they do that now with dogs you know
we start tomorrow
actually.

Ohhhhh says the second guess you won't say how you got **that.**

At the exit I'm behind her.
There tethered to a parking meter is
George. He gets to his feet.
His tail signals reciprocity.
Over his black lip a thread of spittle slides viscid slippery
almost to the pavement hangs there catches the light
gleams feral.

She takes hold of the leash.
Off trots George at heel.

iii. the tongue

John leads me to his water garden, makes coffee
goes back and forth in his bare
feet fetching bagels and jam and cheese.
While he's in the house his large
golden dog sits up to the table
opens its mouth and allows to slither forth a miraculous long tongue
which lollops and slobbers across the white cloth
to where cubes of orange cheese repose on a blue china plate.
The tongue effortlessly coats all visible planes
of that cheese, performs for me a drooling
bow and bundles itself away.

John and I have breakfast, he helping
himself liberally to all that is spread before us, I eating
only a bagel spread with jam.

A warm wind patters among the birch leaves.
A damselfly checks her sheen in the water garden.
I admire the orange cheese, how it glistens in the morning sun.

iv. weimaraner

Consort of the star performer
he takes his seat on stage beside her.
Muscular, short-haired
curves and workings of his body
visible, withers and brisket
hock and cock. His fine coat
changes colour the way grass does
when the wind blows clouds over the sun
not grey not fawn not olive green, a riverine
medley of the three. Sage
maybe. On stage he does not move
a nail, quivers to each note, each voice
each pause. The real star
for me. His eyes never leave
his lady as she speaks her poetry;
they stream fidelity.
The listener a poet longs for.
The lover a woman dreams of.

v. this dog of yours

you and me alone in your house cause my old man's
down east and your old lady's out with the girls and
you and me have work to do and your old lady suggested
I come but you forgot to tell your dog that part
this dog of yours that would die for you
he's checking me out real well every time you turn
your back that nose of his that tongue
right where no lady allows on such short
acquaintance I haven't got near enough hands to brush
him off I follow you he follows me you show me
that painting bullfight red in a clinch with puce frenzy
that painting you planned to hang on my wall
but no your old lady wanted it after all
no doctor looking for lumps ever felt me up
as well as this dog I follow you
down three steps to the small room that was your
book room and now's your bathroom
down boy down three more steps
to the big room that was your den and now's
your book room this dog sleeps with you
his head on the pillow you tell your dog to get lost
I could get lost in this room of yours
he goes up three steps he's got me memorized anyway
the back door knob turns slowly the door opens
and closes stealthily your old lady back so soon
but no it's your dog gently letting himself out
into the sultry August night

Cows

When I am old I will have cows
a few hens, a rooster for the dawn.
I will have cows
the way they bear the sun, the flies
the way their shameless tongues explore
the way the tongues of the young
squish-suck my fingers,
rasp furrows in my cheeks.
I will be embraced
by their need of me morning and evening
bulging udders, teats leaking
invitation. Head braced
by warm curve of cow belly,
that barrel tub of the four stomachs,
ear lulled by cud-steady rhythm,
interior rumble of rumen,
hair dampened by rain-gentle
strings of harvest apple slobber,
I will strip the long teats of each
waiting creature, hands sparing her
the cold embrace of metal mouths
feet ready to evade sudden return
to wildness. Cows will stay with me
stay by me through slow
interior change, recent layers
breaking down to join the dark
impassive silt of long ago.
When I am old I will have cows
a few hens, a rooster for the dawn
that follows.

Hip Man

What makes the engine go?
Desire, desire, desire.
The longing for the dance
Stirs in the buried life.
One season only,
And it's done.

Stanley Kunitz, *Touch Me.*

Hip Man

for Marty

In his poem he says
I saw hips
        I saw hips
   I saw hips
but I know better
cause I went with him to a beach in France
a womb of water warm near shore
cold when you let yourself sink
full fathom five
and as our bare feet moved from grass to hot
sand, he said he liked and didn't like
to come here – groin ache of knowing
he couldn't have what he saw –
for they were sunlove ripe, the breasts of *La Bourgogne*
and no matter which ones I mentioned
he'd seen them first
the pert pair ice-cream cold from deep water
that longed to be licked to a point
the long lazy udders that beckoned like hammocks
and swung like desire in July
the full white mounds tipped with rose grapes
that lolled on the blanket beside us
he claims he's a hip man but I know better, know too
what he'll say when he reads this –
you saw tits
        you saw tits
   you saw tits.

Every Living Minute

for John Terpstra, June 2004.

Sitting with you in a sidewalk
café in Montreal
on a June day, watching wisps of poplar fluff web themselves
in curly hair and belly button rings,
we are playing hooky
from the conference of poets, we are drinking
wine and smoking Gauloises and classifying women's breasts
into types of fruit.

You say being with me is like hanging out with a guy,
you ask if it's a lesbian thing, I say it's an
appreciation of the human body in all its multifarious forms thing.

You don't like them too big, you say, too big makes you feel
scared… or… too responsible.

Right at the height of this, right when the sun is beginning to
somersault and a guy with a saffron python has just
walked by and a long wastrel of reproductive fluff
has draped itself on a pair of passing cantelopes,
you look across at me and say

that if I die first
you're going to read at my funeral.

Yeah, this is what we have in common
you and I and every damn poet in the whole world –
even when we're in Montreal with lollapalooza
tree fluff in our hair,
we can't forget that we are going to die.

Gauloises burn your finger tips, sun burns your nose
the breasts of Montreal burn your vitreous humour –

this is how I'll remember you
and if **you** die first, I'll read

Giants, how only a few thousand years ago
they sat their giant hinds on the escarpment
dangling their feet into freefall, skipping stones across the bay.

It's those lines of yours

They loved it here.
I'm telling you, they absolutely loved
every living minute here

and they regretted ever having to leave.

Six Months

for JSP

In January, my mother dies.

In February, you lend me your books.
The space beneath their words
the silence between them
is caressed by a pencil
guided by your hand
stars of your creation
decorate their skies
your handwriting explores their open spaces.

In March, you invite me
to write in your books, your books
in my kitchen, my living room
on the floor of my car, on the chair
by my bed. I read them
write in them, underline
add my stars to their skies
lean against their tree trunks
lose myself in their forests,
in March, my father dies.

In April, I take you upstairs
to the room left behind by my daughter
the room I made over this winter
and lined with my books.
I show you photos of Armand
who lived to be one hundred
a man happy in pipe smoke
father to my father.

In May, I lend you my books.

In June, you lend me your father
a man of decades and stories,
face inscribed by listening and years
of ministering, to sit by his side is to sit
once again in the circles of pipe smoke.

In July, I ask you with my eyes
to write in my books.

Books

for JSP

I knew that you read
with your teeth, knew
that your heart and your guts
were at risk each time
you opened a book, knew
that without your books
you could not live long.

Today in your room
we pore over words
you've cut from your books
passages pasted on luscious
sheets – cherry and lemon
chartreuse and lime,
chestnut and russet and grape.

I knew that you wrote
in your books, knew
that you underlined and
made stars, knew that you
urged me to write in them
looked for my notes
when I gave them back.

I did not know
you would cut into their flesh
cut out their hearts
excise what you wanted
compose a new order
on cherry and lemon
chestnut, chartreuse and lime.

Letter-Meditation By Water

for TM

Where you are, it is always tomorrow.

I have come here to the shores of Lake Ontario because it is by water
that I feel closest to you.

Here, the light is just beginning to make the void visible.
There, tomorrow's dusk softens the mountain
you see from your window.

In the willow to my left, a cardinal hammers a tropical
recitative, though this is a temperate country.
In the shallows to my right, a vertical shimmer of thinnest grey-blue
raises one long pencil leg, then the other;
his dainty step disturbs not by merest shiver
the mirror he stands in.

Yesterday, a Symphony Pastorale –
smooth lullaby country, amble of sunny interval
jackknife slivers among slate cloud bundles,
thunder, plummet of pressure, rain then sun then rain again,
each drop a half-cup of water.

Yesterday, a poem
brought your marriage crashing down.

It is night-time where you are.
I hope you are asleep on your boat.
I hope you are drifting among the little islands.
I hope you have found a temporary peace upon the water.

Last night the wind tore holes in my sleep, shrieked in the trees
leapfrogged through the house slammed shutters and doors
knocked vases onto floors, made scattered rain
spatter of my papers, my drafts of that poem.

This morning the mirror seems mirage, so still it lies.

You, far away upon the winter waters, you could enter every
locked letter-box of my heart and find nothing not
already opened to you.

A Child Made Of Snow

for Gordon

Aquin said something very beautiful that evening:
'Faisons un enfant de la neige.'

and you said something more beautiful
it was after our picnic lunch far up the park
where wide trees brood over nests of grey grass
and the air has the zing of champagne
you were taking me home
but first we'd stopped at the bookstore
where you bent to pick a book from the shelf
your hands smoothed its jacket its leaf edge
uncut unturned unread
it was then you said it
The book we've worked on together
will be our child
nine months on your shelf nine months on mine
we'll live through its pages write in its margins
leave one another notes
beneath its sleeves and when we are together
we will tender it back and forth

more beautiful because a child made of snow
can live only in air so cold it burns your throat
will vanish at the first stir of spring's wand
but our child will live on and on yes it will leap with its feet of good
tidings like a hart upon the mountain
long after you and I are dust in the mouth of the earth

One Incarnation

for Giorgio

You are all verticals today
A church spire, your
Body a charged wire
On the rack that runs
Between heaven and hell.
No horizontal planes to your
Psyche or soma, an
Icon by El Greco, all
Anguished angularity.
When you rise to read, the
Wide, deep collar of your
Shirt stands tall, chafes your
Earlobes into starch.
God cranks. The Devil cranks.
You grow thinner
And thinner
Bound for
Allegory.

In A Felled Tree

for John Terpstra

You have made a cross from a tree
and it hangs behind you
as you read your poem in fourteen parts.
Above you hangs the concrete cross
that's always in this church.
You noticed your cross
in the shape of a tree
that was part of an orchard
destroyed for a mall, and is now the subject
of your poem for every station of the cross.

Her torso curves like a crescent moon
this cross you found in a tree
who hangs behind you as you read.
You have stripped her of her bark
rubbed her body so it shines oak gold.
Where her arms join her torso,
a knothole. Below,
a schism runs to her feet,
her arms point east and west.
Near the wrist, her left arm becomes two
diverges like the path in the yellow wood.

As you read she begins to move
this cross you found in a felled
tree, moves her body
to your cadence. Her arms beckon
the east, beckon the west.
The split that runs from knothole down
becomes a stream, vineyards appear
on its banks *and the vines*
with the tender grape give a good smell.
All eyes are on her. Behind you
she is leafing green and gold.

Pilgrimage To Prades

On the last day of January 1915, under the sign of the Water Bearer,
in a year of a great war, and down in the shadow of some French
mountains on the borders of Spain, I came into the world.
                                                    – Thomas Merton

Whether the sun is in the dazzle sky of showoff blue
        or the moon is in the boudoir sky of throbbing black

whether crazy sidewalks hopscotch to the end of town
        or tilt towards the green valley

whether poppies shout from the orange ditches
        or Spain thrums behind lavender mountains

whether Christ bleeds marble from His forehead
        or sidewalks flaunt a coprophiliac's delight

whether breadsticks poke insouciant from baskets
        or tatterdemalions flap at birds in orchards

whether blue coos of mourning doves
        taupe dog waggle
                purple tantrums of church bells
        wanton tablecloths hullaballooning on clotheslines
orange cats curled among loaves in sunshine ~

no matter the revelation
        it holds the seeds
of your contemplation.

Alchemy

and I see how in the sway
of things
I am blessed
                    – John B. Lee

On a towel you tore from the roll of paper for wiping
spills, you wrote your results.

Your chemistry teacher, an unrelated Mr. Lee,
his neck a turkey jerk of thinning

fury, ripped it senseless, reprimanded
you. You marched to a different

destiny, hot-drummed a path
to the office and dropped the course, your life

till then pointed towards doctor of animals.
Thus you escaped a future mired

in *the large, showy vulvas of cows*
a life of standing in fundamental shit that steamed

and sweated literal rank, for you were born
to swim through dreamscapes, to high-dive

into poems, heedless of hidden rocks
beneath the surface, born to

metaphor, born to exhale metaphor with every out-
breath, born to a life that spins straw dust into gold

motes, reveals the light in matter, the light
in shit, muck, cows, age, disgruntled sons, careless lovers

the light that loves us.

My Dear,

No, I did not fall in love with Laszlo.

He ate a pork chop that I did not want
in three bites. It was a large pork chop.
He took a small, sharp knife
cut the chop into three triangles
left the border of glistening fat on the meat.
He ate each triangle in quick succession, chewed each
only two or three times before gulping it down.
That pork chop disappeared in the time it would take
you to say, "Budapest is the capital of Hungary."
Like you, I fall in love easily.
But I could not fall in love
with a man so unabashedly carnivorous
a man whose esophagus
could withstand an isosceles triangle
scraping over the delicate membranes
a man whose neck bulged with its unseemly load
as a snake bulges while gorging a rat.

Perhaps I am a little more fastidious than I like to think.

You asked me this question last May.
The answer emerged
from the deep blue underside of my mind
only this morning
floated on the surface all day
among the flotsam and jetsam of work.

Yours on an evening of glacial cold,

    M.

The Listener

Later, when he's taken
my history
and I'm sitting on the table naked
under the white paper coat
and he's bent to my chest
bent to the language he knows best of all,
he must use his hand to lift up
my heavy, hanging breast
so he can listen beneath.
Sorry, he whispers
and again *Sorry*, as he grasps it
more firmly, lifts it higher,
his breath a gentle stir against my skin.
It's okay, I whisper back, trying to think
what to say to put him at ease,
this man whose calling it is
to lay open the human heart,
but deciding, in the end, that it's better
to stay quiet
to let this small hand, these ears
touch and listen
                    touch and listen
better to let them cross my chest as if
picking their way across the stepping
stones of a summer creek where it slows
in the shallows, the hidden life beneath
barely disturbing the surface.

Now You Are Mostly Gold And Blue

I want you to fill your hands with the mud, like a blessing.

Mary Oliver, *Rice*.

The Farm Your Lover

to my father

She came to you on a bright scudding morning of spring
faint scent of damp earth
the promise of summer.

She came with the long, light days in her skirts
burst into your life with the force of a
green stem splitting cement
from below.

She came from rose soil combed fine
ready to receive the seed.

She came to you barefoot, through buttercups and feather grass
through pasture still wet from the creek's spring floods
her ankles untouched by coarse dark spikes
of sword grass that grow there.

Green lace her dress
her hair a tangle of bee hum.

She lasted your lifetime
destroyed your marriage, your health
gave you the only happiness you ever knew.

All around you, quick flitter of bird wing –
the hum, the flick, the dart, the skimming, swarming intensity.

Spit

My mother said the farm was a curse.
She spat the word "farm"
and the word "curse" the way strangers spit
on the street, the way men with hard eyes
hork and spit without shame. My mother
spat the word farm like that. First, she ran
the small fierce brush of the vacuum
up and down and across the windows
sucking fat buzzing flies by the hundreds
into the tube. Then she scrubbed
by hand with short, jerking swipes
bits of straw, dried shreds of manure, dead
insects, mice droppings, cat hairs, dog hairs
from the kitchen floor. When she spat the words
"farm," and "curse," the words lay there
for my father to see when he came in, finally,
from the barn, sweat and dirt a running paste
on his forehead, his cheeks. He came in wary
and looked at the floor. His eyes lurched away
but not before he had seen the words
the bubbles of spittle that clung to them.
The words lay there, on the floor, between them.
Did not evaporate.

A Tale

to my father

You cartwheeled from house to barn
stood on the hillock and yodeled till the hills shouted,
your hair a halo against my sun.

You placed one hand on the pasture fence
vaulted the top rail, rubber
boots a sudden whirr above me.

You stood on the swing and pumped, took me
so high the tree swayed and shrieked.
Your knees cracked at my ears.

You folded yourself in the wood box
feet tucked against shoulders, double-jointed
arms monkey-busy tossing kindling.

You climbed the tree to the highest branch
held on for the heart-stopping dip
plucked apples beyond human reach.

You somersaulted from the old stone bridge
splashed thunder, sent the water scrambling
up the banks, swam the river all the way to the lake.

You lowered the bucket
into the well. Tap danced on cement
for me and the moon.

When you wanted rain, you reached up and rapped on
clouds, when you wanted sun you rose
in the dark, yanked off the shawls of dawn.

When I tell these stories about you,
my brother and sister, born later,
listen as one listens
to a tale about a stranger.

Leave The Water In

Allowed enough water to cover
her body, she sinks low in the tub
soaks till her hands are shriveled.
Her new breasts and her mound
poke through as islands. In the sea
that surrounds them, she plays
like a seal who risks losing her
skin to a man.

      Leave the water in.
            It is her father.

She steps wet into flannelette.
Outside the door he waits, silently
she brushes by. When she hears
the low groaning squeak
of the enamel, she knows he is lying
flat, as she did, head out of the water
the rest of him wavy in the fluid
that lapped at her. From her bedroom
she hears her body's secrets
nudge his pores
            later, hears the water
circle, protest, submit its lapping sea
to the waiting narrow hole, leaving only
their ring of mixed remains.

Later her mother
    will kneel
scour the ring away.

Father

The red cart pulls the horse
    legs braced, up the hill
though iron shoes tear
    a gash in the road
and travelers wait in the ditches

The red cart weeps sweat
    strains and heaves
Tongue scrapes a long plaint
    wheels blister
tongue rends from groove
    axel screeches
wood cracks, threatens buckle

You've got them backwards, we cry
    but you can't hear us
you're hoarse with urging
    your cart on and up
you've lashed it to blood flakes
    flecked it with spittle
fissured the whole with mute will

Upstairs

to my father

The evening rings with that first green that stirs
the unlived life within,
goldfinch yellow sways from the circle of lawn

to the whistling emerald edge of the forest.
Robins race across the grass,
kildeer and bobolink perform on the high wire.

Upstairs in the southwest corner of the old farmhouse
in the tiny room that has always been yours
you lie on the blue quilt that belonged to your mother.

From upstairs comes an intermittent sound, that vestige
of a voice left you by the disease.
The voice is calling your firstborn.

Years later, I'll remember that this is when
the shapes that weren't there
began to appear to you, that evenings were your worst time.

Sitting with my sister and brother in the evening sun, I ignore
your call. When they can't bear to hear you
any longer, I climb the narrow back stairs to your room

sit on the edge of the chair by your bed.
'What do you want?'

Could you ask them to make less noise?
"Is that why you called me?" I stand to go.

Tell me about your work.
"There's nothing to tell."

I'm not well. Your hand falters towards me.
"I know, I'm sorry, I have to go."

That young woman, full of her own future, how she descended
the back stairs to sit again
like a cat in the spring sun, licking the long length of herself.

Gold And Blue

to my father

Now that your memory is gone
cracked over the knee
of the disease like so much
kindling for the fire,
now that your mind is gone
emptied of its understanding
like a pail of windfalls
thrown to the calves,
now that your spirit is gone
visible only in dreams
like a missing soldier,
now you are mostly gold and blue.

Against the milkweed-silk-white
sheets, your blonde hair shines
like sun-splintered marigolds
strung across the sacred river
as a bridge to the beyond,
your blue eyes a pond
that holds the summer sky
and circles to the final shore.

In fields you fenced I find
buttercup, daisy, primula
goldenrod, cowslip, cinquefoil
bluebell, columbine, bellflower
forget-me-not, chicory, aster.
       kernels under the cornsilk
       smooth curve of the saltlick
Now you are mostly gold and blue.

On Reading Margaret Atwood's
Negotiating With The Dead

to my father

So now I find out that the food of the dead
is round and red
that one should leave food out
for the dead at night, that it may
bring luck or at least
keep one free from harm.
Now I learn that what the dead want most
is blood, that's why
their food is red and heart-
shaped, more or less.

All your life we wondered what it meant –
your mania for apples, strawberries, tomatoes, cherries
the quantities you consumed, the special rules you had
for when you could eat them
only in season
only the reddest
only five minutes between picking and eating,
apples only at nine p.m.
only the ripest, the most plump.
We watched you consume
whole patches of berries
gardens of tomatoes
orchards of apples and cherries,
Tantalus released, boughs big with fruit at last
within your grasp.

Even then, some part of us knew your relentless
insatiable love
of these round red fruits
was not of this world, that you
were laying up for yourself
treasures somewhere else.
And now that I think of it, after your mighty nine p.m. feast
you always left one, red, on the table
a knife beside.

Whom were you feeding, my father, how
did you know, way back then
what I have discovered only today -
that the dead are often hungry and unsatisfied
that the dead do not vanish completely
that we the living owe the dead something
that I owe you
something…
but first, after my nine o'clock feast
an apple
left out overnight
Red Delicious, when I have it,
tall, heart-shaped, an intense brilliant red.

The Strands Of That Fragrance

She moved two chairs in front of the door that opened
into nowhere, into what
she called thin air, so we sat side by side facing out.

It had rained that morning; the front field steamed
in the sun. My mother held
on her lap my doll with the long blonde hair.

There on the second floor, we were so high
we could see the field, the creek
my Uncle's barn, more fields, the woods beyond.

She parted the hair into three strands, began
to weave them into a braid.
Drifting in through the screen, the scent of the pink

peace rose that grew by the rotting front porch.
White cattle grazed
in the wide front field we looked down on;

the sound of their chewing entered with the rose.
My mother placed the doll
on my lap, told me to try. Over and over she waited

as I hesitated, then guided my fingers the right way.
Drifting in, the scent
of sweet vernal-grass, fescue, timothy, clover;

I couldn't have named the strands of that fragrance then.
Sitting together, we worked
till at last I could fashion a clumsy braid.

I don't remember the rest of the day, only
that in the night I awakened,
that the moon shone in like a sun.

That I wondered that night and wonder yet
at the stranger who strayed in that afternoon,
the stranger with patient hands, and time to sit and braid.

Last Story

I still think about it sometimes
the last story my mother told me
before they took her away to open her heart
and brought her back a stranger,
the story a technician told her – that he once found
nestled in that hot moist crease
beneath a woman's breast
a sandwich.
What kind of sandwich, I wondered, what shape
was it in? I knew better than to ask
my mother, knew she'd not only
not have asked the questions
she'd deem me unseemly for thinking them.

When she said sandwich I saw all those years
of doughy white bread spread thin
with margarine, small slivers of ham
pressed flat by her hand
squares of wax paper cut just so
shaped to hold my sandwiches snug.
At school they laughed, of course, at my odd
gluey flat-cakes, theirs had layers of lettuce
cheese and tomatoes, half a package of ham rolled up,
theirs stood high.

I ask myself sometimes – my mother's last story
was it about poverty, was it about
illness, loss of the instinct to groom?
Was it about the appearance of the
strange in unexpected places?
Or was it simply a story about hunger –
a heart colluding with a breast
to trap a sandwich
a heart needing assurance
that sustenance
was right there, just the other side of the skin?

The Spatula

I woke this morning thinking of
your rubber spatula
the one you used when I was a girl,
your white spatula stained dun
pitted and pocked and bubbled
from long use, a step-shaped
piece missing from the corner.

When your spatula was in your hands
its tip flipped from front to back,
fit itself to the curves of your chipped
bowl; your wrist undulated like a child
playing alone in the swells of the sea.
I asked you to stop so I could lick
the bowl; you frowned and persisted
flopped your tool finally
into the soapy water along with
the spoons, handed me what was left.
Once, I put my face right in the bowl
to lap the last batter,
you fished out your spatula, lightly
swatted the crown of my head.

This is the first you've visited me
since you died, the first
I've seen of you in four years, and even now
you didn't come yourself, you sent
your spatula, sent it instead
or maybe on ahead.
When I awoke this morning, found it there
on the threshold, I took it in my hands,
gave it my face to rasp.

Flora's Bread

In December, my mother's sister baked her last
loaves, lay down and died in her sleep.

The crust of the bread was burnt
its form was fallen, misshapen.

That Christmas, my mother asked me –
Would you take some of Flora's bread?

I have her last batch in my freezer;
would you take two loaves of her bread?

No thanks, I told her
I have my own.

Would you like just one loaf?
Flora made it.

No thanks. I have my own bread.
I don't eat other kinds.

The next year, like her sister
my mother died in December.

That night, I dreamed
of Flora's bread.

In the dream
I bowed my head

kissed the burnt crust
broke, tasted, savoured,

asked of its scarred breadth
forgiveness.

Knowing Only Now Why I Asked

to my mother

There was a question I asked you over and over
when I was a child.
If our house burned down
and you could save only one thing
what would it be?
You never hesitated
replied as if you were being asked
for the first time. The frowns
your forehead harboured
diminished, a slip of light entered
your restless eyes of green and brown
as if you were seeing something I couldn't
a dream of shining water, maybe.
Your words always the same.
Oh, I'd save the old, black photo
album, the one that begins
the day I brought you home.

In your eightieth year, after the open heart
surgery, after your heart stopped
for too long
and they brought you back to the ward
a stranger
I asked what you saw
between this world and the next
and instantly your face became
a face I knew
the face that told me all those years ago
no matter how often I asked
what you would save from the flames.

Dear God

Let it be twilight, for only then do you paint like Matisse.

Let the sky's daring be a raving chromatic red, daubs of orange and carmine.
    Let Kiri be singing *O mio babbino caro.*
        Let the speed of my car be one hundred and eighty k.

Let the car become an F18, let it leave the earth.

Give me a second or two to understand the levitation
    as inevitable
        so I may add to it my power
            my submission.

And in the years before this event
    roll me, oh God
        roll me in the glorious mess of life
            the guts the mud the smite the blood the song the sob
                of life.

Roll me as I roll the dough of the leavened bread.
Knead me, God.
        Pummel me.
            Press me thin.

Set me to rise in warm places,
    use me, use me
        use me up

so that when the flying is over, when the crash comes,
    your fire has only my crumbs
        to burn

for the rest of me has sown itself into your world
    into every little crevice and rock face
        into each particular heartscape
            of this fallen world.

Domesticity

Our homes...are where the action is;
they are where the riches of experience are distributed.

Janet Malcolm, ***Reading Chekhov.***

The Marriage

i. still life

Thank you for the gift of your
buxom zucchini
shaped like a butternut squash
skin mottled olive and yellow cream.
I could not bear to eat her.

Therefore I laid your zucchini
beside my banana
thinking to create still life of her
that curving, earth mother hip
the defining arc
of my composition.

Right away it was clear
how much they had in common
your rotund zucchini and my banana,
that polyphony of green and yellow
those cylindrical torsos
that purposeful, concave thrust
away from stem,
a tacitness so deep
one may never
get to the bottom of it.

ii. imprint

With you I riverswim
deeper than I'd go alone
down past furl and dapple
gurgle and babble
tickle of minnow
playful shadow
down to weight
we struggle to descend
into and through, down to
where throats burn
and the river's clenched
fists boom
against our ears, down to
where our palms gain at last
the imprint of the river bed

from where,
chasing the bubbles
of our escaping
life, we ascend
hands a prow of prayer.
Poseidon roused
and at our heels
we burst free, step onto land
palms up palms open palms inscribed
psalms of the river's deepest places.

iii. fire

They did not steal it from the gods;
they had it installed.
Their living room faces north, has been cold
all the years of the marriage.

Before long, they spend their days with it,
they bake, lounge, loll. Siesta is long
aspirations cold, remote, impossible.
Books on their chests, they slumber,
all that matters, the creature comfort of this steady
warmth, this flame. The cats have loosened
their wintertime tucks and balls and curls,
lie now summertime long.

Nights, her husband goes up to the cold bedroom,
she rolls herself in an old afghan,
learns the language of the fire,
its sharp retorts and windy roars, its hissings
and sputterings, its little shifts and settlings.
Dreams of her ancestors around the fire of their night
those sacred fire-tenders of old, who knew
not to allow the fire to go out.

iv. deep in the hold

Dinner plates unscraped
upon the table, they went
to bed, fell asleep after love.
In the night, she awakens,
wedged between him and
the dog, the three of them
naked, breathing in tandem;
they are deep in the hold
of a small ship, anchored
near shore, nested under
flannelette, rocked by
unfathomed life beneath.

Along the dock, half-
smothered by wind and distance,
rough cries in other languages,
bottles breaking, lives confined
to port shattering,
but in their hidden cabin,
they breathe and breathe
the three of them
two sleeping, one awake,
their breaths retreating then returning
like the sea.

v. after watching in-line skaters on the Bayfront trail

It looks effortless for him
    a lying back on the furred paths of the wind
his only motion slight tilt from side to side

She thrashes and flails
    a red heart beats in her cheeks
her strokes unpredictable

Spandex-suited greyhound
    he slices the air with his stride
 lean, bent almost double

hands cupped behind his back
    pose of the learned lecturer
whose words seduce

Later, it is she who lies back in invisible arms
    each stroke a note held so long
that it carries the intimation of no return

vi. i am not ironing linen

The iron is hot
The dial up
past *perma press*
      past *steam*
            past *wool*
                  past *cot*

resting on *lin*.

I am not ironing linen.

I am striking
      branding
            gouging

expressive charring rents
      in your shirt

      charred eyes
           to curl and smolder

jagged tears.

vii. gift

A full bin
of half-cooked compost
your parting gift
to me

as I deconstruct
the layers
a last
intimacy

pierced kernels
on gnawed cobs
trees of
broccoli

thin worms
shiny-peeled
like birds
one day old

and last
where I can barely
reach to scoop
dark gold.

Her Daffodil Hair Flies with the Spring

i. two

at the African Lion Safari

Something had displeased
you, in your window seat
you faced straight ahead
would look neither left nor right.
An ostrich ran beside the bus
its head level with your window
its head turned towards you
its eyes fixed on you
it ran precisely beside you
tethered by cords invisible
to us. It was August
the sun a thorn on my neck
the soft thud of a knowledge
I did not want, its pads
approaching.
Father, mother, sister:
Meredith, please, look at the ostrich
look, it's running as fast as the bus
look, it's running right beside you
look, see how it wants you to look.

Your eyes fixed on distance
the ice sculpture set to your shoulders
the hard sheen of your mute profile
the sparks of blue light that slivered off you
the feathered wide-eyed running creature desperate
for your human gaze.

ii. nine

She has begun wondering
about infinity
is trying to wrap herself around the idea
of there being
no end
is letting her mind slip on and on through the earth to China
past Heaven and Hell and the birth of Christ
past Adam and Eve and the apes past the galaxies on and on and on
never ending ever – how far would that be?
Every now and then
she falls through black space
the hours rushing in her ears at the speed of
forever
this time she will keep falling world without end her braids fly long and straight
her stomach crashes against her heart the miles of her intestines stream loose

Something always brings her back.
Clang of her mother's iron on metal plate
hiss on wind-battered cloth
steady tick of the kitchen clock.

For ever lets her go
for now.

iii. eleven

she hangs by her heels
from the horns of the crescent moon
strides from star to star

she rolls with the thunder clouds
over the park
gull-screams the claps

she slides down bright cuts
in the riven sky
eyes open to the gash

she swings on the high wires
in the puddles of sky
after the rain

her daffodil hair flies with the spring
her guffaw
shatters window panes

iv. twelve

Flute and piccolo poke
from her backpack
as she sets off for rehearsal
this Saturday dawn;
she does not see me
in the garden clipping rosa
damascena.

When she was born
her face was familiar
I'd seen it
each time musicians passed
each time musicians tuned
each time exquisite dissonance
announced performance.

Now Saturday softens to dusk
as I pull to the gutter
pails heavy with gardens past
while under her fingers
Fantaisie-Impromptu
lifts off the keyboard,
allegro agitato
ascends through the open window
charges the dusk that blurs me
with the charmed particles
that preceded her into this world.

v. fourteen

Last week
she strode
steel-toed across
her bedroom
floor.
Yesterday
she flung
iron pans
clang
at the spiders
that hung
from her walls.
Today
fists of thunder
pound doors
sunder
the timbers
of roof beams
Today
she cracks
open the rafters
I swing from.

vi. seventeen

She comes home and tells us her name
is Welsh
and means *from the sea*
and the old Welsh woman who told her
says it a different way
the accent on the second e
Merèdith.

Merèdith, I say, Merèdith, trying it out,
this new name, and as I say it as mantra
Merèdith Merèdith
she seems to shimmer and slowly reveal
a part of herself I've never seen
a part finned and lithe
her long straight hair now hung with weeds
and plucked by combs of the deep
the grace of her bones backlit by the moon.
I call her new name – Merèdith Merèdith,
as waving now she flows from our lives on an unseen tide.

Mèredith, I call, and she's here
in the brown chair by the fireplace,
fingers deep in the thick tiger coat of her kitten.

vii. nineteen

On her first hot day home in Ontario
she crashes the province, yes –
six foot Valkyrie frame, blue bangs, she strides
the mall in combat
boots, me minioned in her wake.
Her chunky handcuff-bracelets, chain at her neck
that threatens throttle, pierced eyebrow, nose, lip, chin –
all draw skittish looks of quick alarm
from white-haired folk and young suburban mothers
pushing strollers. The claw that protrudes
from her lower lip, the shards she shoots from those
blue eyes silence chittering salesgirls
as surely as a sudden bolt from Zeus.

It's no surprise, then, when cash
registers clang their last, fan blades
shudder to impotence, phones cease, shoppers stop
to watch as silence and darkness descend with spread wings.
Whadja do that for? I whisper
in the direction of her six-ringed ear.
Just a sudden whim, she allows
dropping me a rare goddess wink.
Our slow trip home through traffic mayhem
is hot but she will not relent, will not
turn the power back on.

That night, she dribbles and thunks a basketball
through candlelit dining room and kitchen darkness
despite my pleas she stop,
fights with her boyfriend in high voltage French
of which I do not understand a word
but *bagatelle*. Every room strewn with her garments
the necessities of her hours, a sudden sweaty
jungle taking shape around me;

82

this boisterous burgeoning creature
is my replacement on the planet;
she leafs out in tropical vegetation,
casts surreal shadows on my walls,
her juicy expansionist corolla sucks in
the withering peduncle of my life

as I cook, pick up socks, re-stock re-stock re-stock.

viii. twenty-three

The maples have given over their sap
when she returns
after four years away.
The maples have unfolded their leaves
when she returns
with enough to fill a small house.
The maples are dropping their keys
as she tries
to fit herself back into her old room.

The papery sails of the keys
float their round wombs to the warm earth.
She brings her boyfriend to the hearth.
There I am already.

The rhubarb uncrinkles
the birch dangles its wind chimes.
She goes to the kitchen to make herself dinner.
There I am already.

The earthworms haul thin brown leaves
along soil-soft burrows.
She goes looking for a job.
There I am already.

Her hair is a thick, burnished tangle
her sap rises
her buds break.

ix. twenty-six

She brought home her grown up woman's
heart that Christmas
brought it home in pieces.
In between baking and playing cards
in between presents and feasting
I held the pieces in my lap, out of sight
beneath an apron or an afghan
and as we talked, my hands turned
the pieces this way and that
seeking to find how they fit.

One evening, as we sat by the fire
her hair falling over her silent face
my hands a mudra of turning,
I thought how she'd been long ago
at my breast
how the arc of my milk
spanned her young sky with the promise
how the covenant between us
broke the light into fingers
of colour.

I wore my fingertips raw that Christmas
turning and turning those
separate pieces, unable to give her, her last
day at home, a heart good as new.
When I kissed her goodbye
for another year and turned back
to the house, it was to glimpse
her once more as she'd been in those days,
how the arc of plenty had curved her way,
how the rain had dropped gentle
on all living creatures.

The Writer

In the washroom
cubicle of the
Primrose Hotel
on Jarvis
releasing my waters
to the underground
river
I tilt my head
backwards

discover
the ceiling to be
a mirror
vast and dark
and there in that mirror
a row of strangers
heads bowed
cell upon cell of
stygian figures
bent to their work
my upturned face
alone among bowed heads
seeing
as a god sees

Notes

The final two lines of the title poem *The Life of the Four Stomachs* are from Mary Oliver's poem *Wild Geese* in her **New and Selected Poems**.

The final two lines of *Pilgrimage to Prades* are a reference to Thomas Merton's book **New Seeds of Contemplation**.

The italicized lines in *Alchemy ~ the large showy vulvas of cows* and *the light that loves us* – are from the *oeuvre* of John B. Lee.

The italicized lines *and the vines with the tender grape/give a good smell*, quoted in *In a Felled Tree*, are from the **King James Version of the Bible**, *Song of Solomon*, 2, 13.

The epigraph in *A Child Made of Snow* is from **HA! A Self-Murder Mystery** by Gordon Sheppard.

Dear God: Stan White brought to the Hamilton Poetry Centre workshop a poem about his hoped-for way of dying and inspired others to write their own "Dear God" poems.

These poems have appeared in this or another form, in some cases under different titles, in the following publications:

Two was a runner up in **Arc**'s Poem of the Year contest and appeared in **Grain**. *On Reading Margaret Atwood's Negotiating with the Dead* was an Honourable Mention in **Room of One's Own** 2003 poetry contest. *Vulva is the Latin Word for Ditch* appeared in **The Malahat Review**; *This Dog of Yours* in **Grain**; *Why would Garrison Keillor Wash his Hands Ever?* in **Matrix**; *Twenty-eight* in the anthology **Body Language** edited by John B. Lee; *Six Months* in **The Windsor Review**; *The Strands of that Fragrance, Knowing Only Now Why I Asked, Spit, Pea Season*, and *In a Felled Tree* in **The Antigonish Review**; *Understanding T.S. Eliot at Last* in **Prairie Fire**; *Cows* in **The Amethyst Review**; *I Am Not Ironing Linen* in **Other Voices**; *Letter Meditation by Water, Hip Man* and *The Life of the Four Stomachs* in **Hammered Out**.

Acknowledgements

A special thank you

to Marty Gervais of Black Moss Press, for his work on behalf of Canadian writers, for his books and art photographs, for his mentorship to so many and his creation of community, and for the fun literary events he masterminds; to his talented editor Jon Flieger; to J. S. Porter, *mon semblable, mon frère*; to the Little Workshop: Linda Frank, Bernadette Rule, Jeffery Donaldson and John Terpstra for their friendship and invaluable help, to Linda especially for the one-on-ones; to John B. Lee, for his two ships: mentor and friend; to the workshop participants of the Hamilton Poetry Centre; to the accomplished students of McMaster University's Writing Program; to the London workshop group who make it worth the drive; to Bryan Prince Bookseller and Staff, for their store that is home, their work for the writing community of Hamilton; to Gordon Sheppard, for his love and encouragement during the final year and a half of his life.

to my fellow traveling poets and readers at *Shakespeare and Company* in Paris, fellow sojourners *chez* Howard and Jeannette Aster at *La Roche d'Hys*, to Marty for making France happen – *merci à tous, c'était magnifique*; to Wendy Morton and the Random Acts of Poetry Group, especially to Marty, John B. and Mary Ann Mulhern – it was a random blast!

to TM, without whom nothing.

Dan Pilling and Marie Gear Cerson – to you the most heartfelt thanks of all, always.

MEMBRE DU GROUPE SCABRINI

Québec, Canada
2006